J398.20948 BRA
Braun, Eric, 1971- author
Loki

Gods of Legend

LOKI

ERIC BRAUN

Black Rabbit Books

J398.
20948
BRA

Bolt is published by Black Rabbit Books
P.O. Box 3263, Mankato, Minnesota, 56002.
www.blackrabbitbooks.com
Copyright © 2018 Black Rabbit Books

Marysa Storm, editor; Michael Sellner, designer;
Omay Ayres, photo researcher

All rights reserved. No part of this book may be reproduced, stored in a retrieval system, or transmitted in any form or by any means, electronic, mechanical, photocopying, recording, or otherwise, without written permission from the publisher.

Library of Congress Cataloging-in-Publication Data
Names: Braun, Eric, 1971- author.
Title: Loki / by Eric Braun.
Description: Mankato, Minnesota : Black Rabbit Books, [2018] | Series: Bolt. Gods of legend | Includes bibliographical references and index. | Audience: Age 9-12. | Audience: Grade 4 to 6.
Identifiers: LCCN 2016049942 (print) | LCCN 2016058511 (ebook) | ISBN 9781680721386 (library binding) | ISBN 9781680722024 (e-book) | ISBN 9781680724479 (paperback)
Subjects: LCSH: Loki (Norse deity)–Juvenile literature. | Mythology, Norse–Juvenile literature.
Classification: LCC BL870.L6 B73 2018 (print) | LCC BL870.L6 (ebook) | DDC 398.209368/01–dc23
LC record available at https://lccn.loc.gov/2016049942

Printed in the United States at CG Book Printers,
North Mankato, Minnesota, 56003. 3/17

Image Credits

Alamy: Collection Christophel, 28; Ellion, 17 (woman); INTERFOTO, 20; Ivy Close Images: 4–5, 6 (both) 15, 23; Commons.wikimedia.org: Louis Huard / Adam Cuerden, 12 (bottom); W.G. Collingwood, 9 (bottom); Independent Artist: Mauricio Herrera, Cover, 27; iStock: berdsigns, 10; whitemay, 29; The Johnson Galleries: Howard David Johnson, 19, 24–25; Shutterstock: alphabe, 16 (salmon); Catmando, 9 (top); dezi, 16 (mare); grib_nick, 17 (fly); Molodec, 1, 32; Patthana Nirangkul, 16–17 (falcon); Ralf Juergen Kraft, 31; Vuk Kostic, 3, 12 (top), Back Cover
Every effort has been made to contact copyright holders for material reproduced in this book. Any omissions will be rectified in subsequent printings if notice is given to the publisher.

CONTENTS

CHAPTER 1
An Ancient Story......4

CHAPTER 2
Norse Mythology......8

CHAPTER 3
Loki's Children........18

CHAPTER 4
Becoming Cruel.......26

Other Resources..........30

CHAPTER 1

An ANCIENT Story

The trickster Loki lived with the gods. He did not like the gods very much. But he did enjoy playing tricks on them. Over time, he began to dislike the gods more and more. His pranks became crueler too. The trick he played on Balder was the worst of them all.

5

6

A Deadly Trick

Balder was a kind god. His mother wanted to protect him. She made everything in the world promise not to hurt Balder. But she didn't ask the **mistletoe** plant. Loki discovered her mistake. He went to a blind god. He tricked him into shooting a sharpened mistletoe branch at Balder. The branch pierced Balder. It killed him instantly.

Loki was called "Trickster." He was also called "Sly One" and "Shape Changer."

CHAPTER 2

Norse MYTHOLOGY

The story of Loki is a Norse **myth**. **Ancient** people told stories to explain the world. Many of their stories were about gods. Norse people believed the gods lived among them. They believed in other magical creatures too.

Norse people lived in northern Europe from the 700s to about 1100. Vikings were Norse warriors.

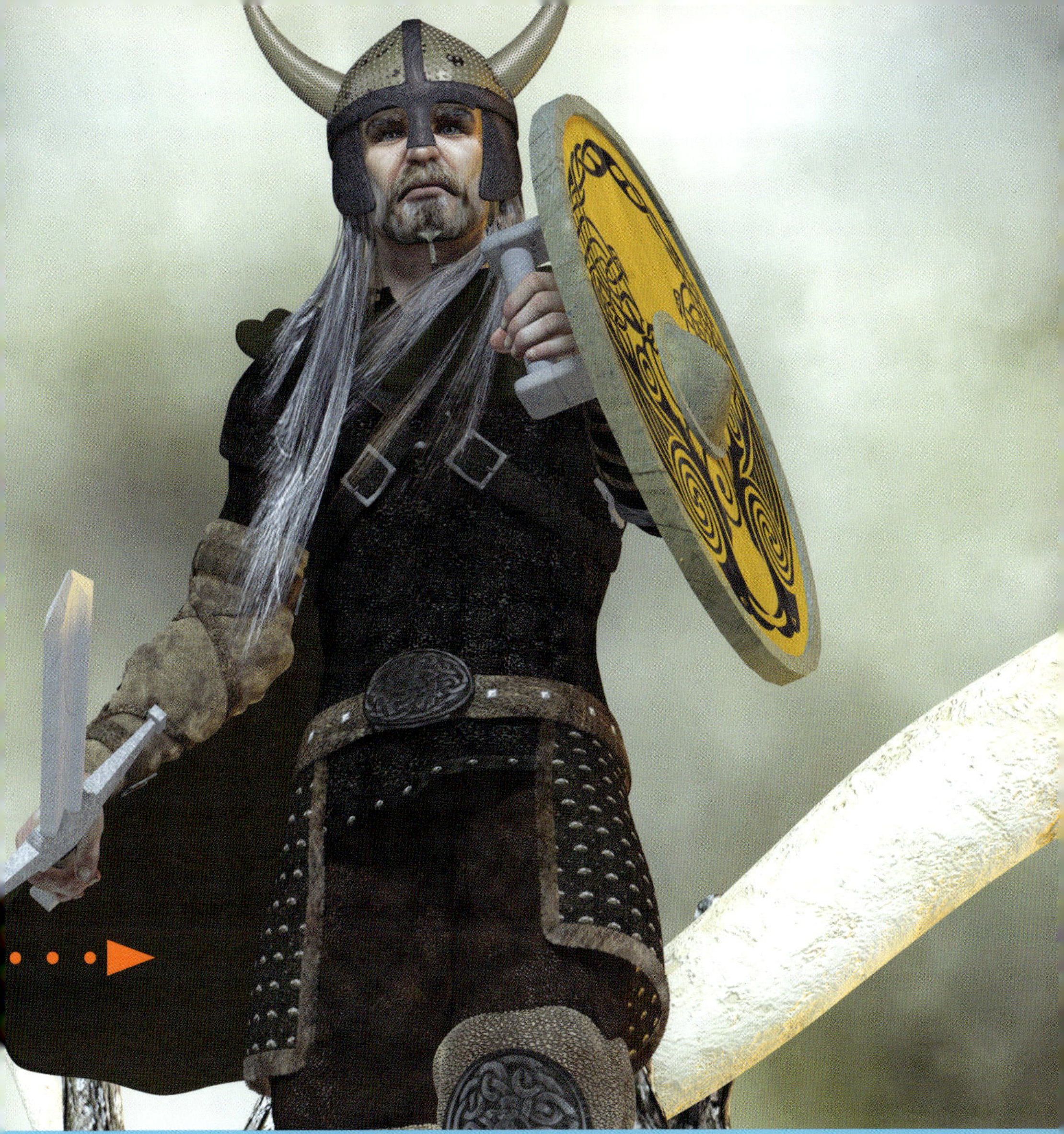

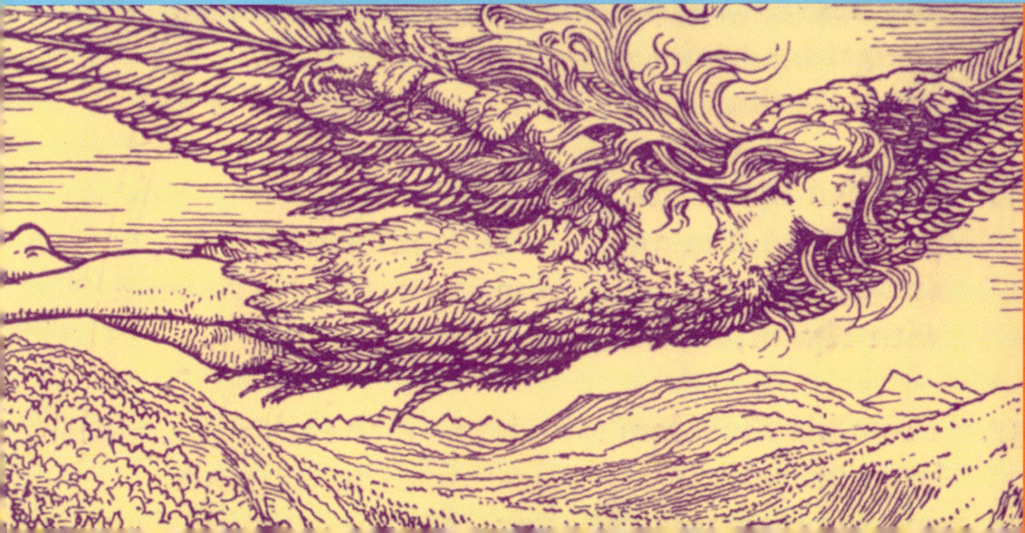

THE WORLD OF THE ANCIENT NORSE

Vikings came from what is now **Norway**, **Sweden**, and **Denmark**. They spread their beliefs to other places.

GREENLAND

ICELAND

IRELAND

UNITED KINGDOM

RUSSIA

GERMANY

FRANCE

The gods punished Loki for his tricks. They once tied him to a rock beneath a snake. The snake's **venom** dripped on Loki. The venom hurt him. The pain caused Loki to shake the earth.

Trickster

Some stories say Loki was half god and half giant. Others say he was just a giant. Giants and gods were usually enemies. But the gods let Loki live with them. Loki did not care about the gods, though. He played tricks that caused them trouble.

Shape-Shifter

Loki could change his **appearance**. He could be a man or woman. He could even be an animal. This ability helped him trick others.

Loki once changed his appearance to keep Balder dead. After he died, Balder went to the **underworld**. A leader there said there was a way to bring Balder back. If every living thing **wept** for him, Balder could return. Everything but a giantess cried. The giantess was Loki in disguise.

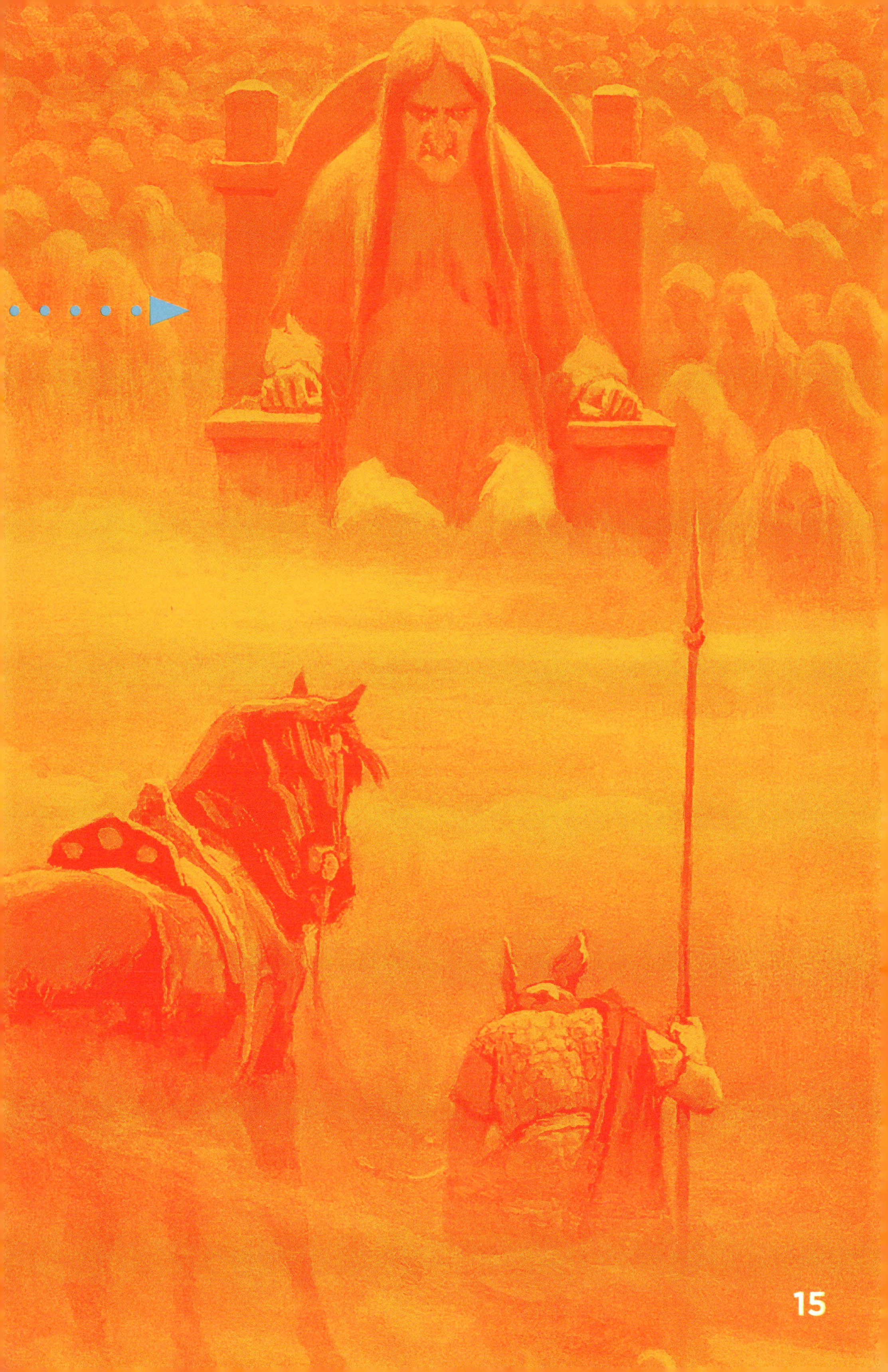

MARE

FALCON

SALMON

FORMS LOKI TOOK

Stories say Loki changed into many things.

OLD WOMAN

FLY

CHAPTER 3

Loki's Children

Stories say Loki had many children. In one story, Loki turned into a mare. He gave birth to a magical horse. It had eight legs. It could travel over sea and sky. The horse was faster than all other horses. Loki gave the horse to Odin.

Odin was leader of the Norse gods. Balder was Odin's son.

19

Stories say one of Loki's tricks will cause the final battle. In it, he will side with the giants. The battle is supposed to destroy the world.

Midgard Serpent

Another one of Loki's children was a huge snake. The gods feared it was evil. So Odin sank the snake beneath the sea. The snake grew until it circled the world of the humans and giants.

Norse stories say there will be a final battle. In it, the gods and giants will fight. Nearly everyone will die. The snake will kill Thor, the thunder god.

Hel and Fenrir

Loki also fathered a giant wolf named Fenrir. Stories say Fenrir will kill Odin during the final battle.

Loki had a daughter too. Her name was Hel. Half of her body was beautiful. The other half was dead. Odin put her in the underworld. There, she watched over the dead.

Loki and Angrboda's Children

Loki had three children with the giantess Angrboda.

FENRIR

HEL

MIDGARD SERPENT

YGGDRASIL

The Norse believed the **universe** had three levels. The levels were part of a giant tree. The tree was called Yggdrasil (IG-druh-sil).

MIDDLE LEVEL
where humans and giants live

TOP LEVEL
where the gods live

RAINBOW BRIDGE
connects top level to middle level

LOWER LEVEL
the underworld

CHAPTER 4

Becoming CRUEL

Some myths are about Loki's early life. In those stories, his tricks are more playful. For example, he cuts off a goddess' hair. But in stories of his later life, Loki is much meaner. His tricks become harmful.

> In early myths, Loki sometimes helped the gods.

27

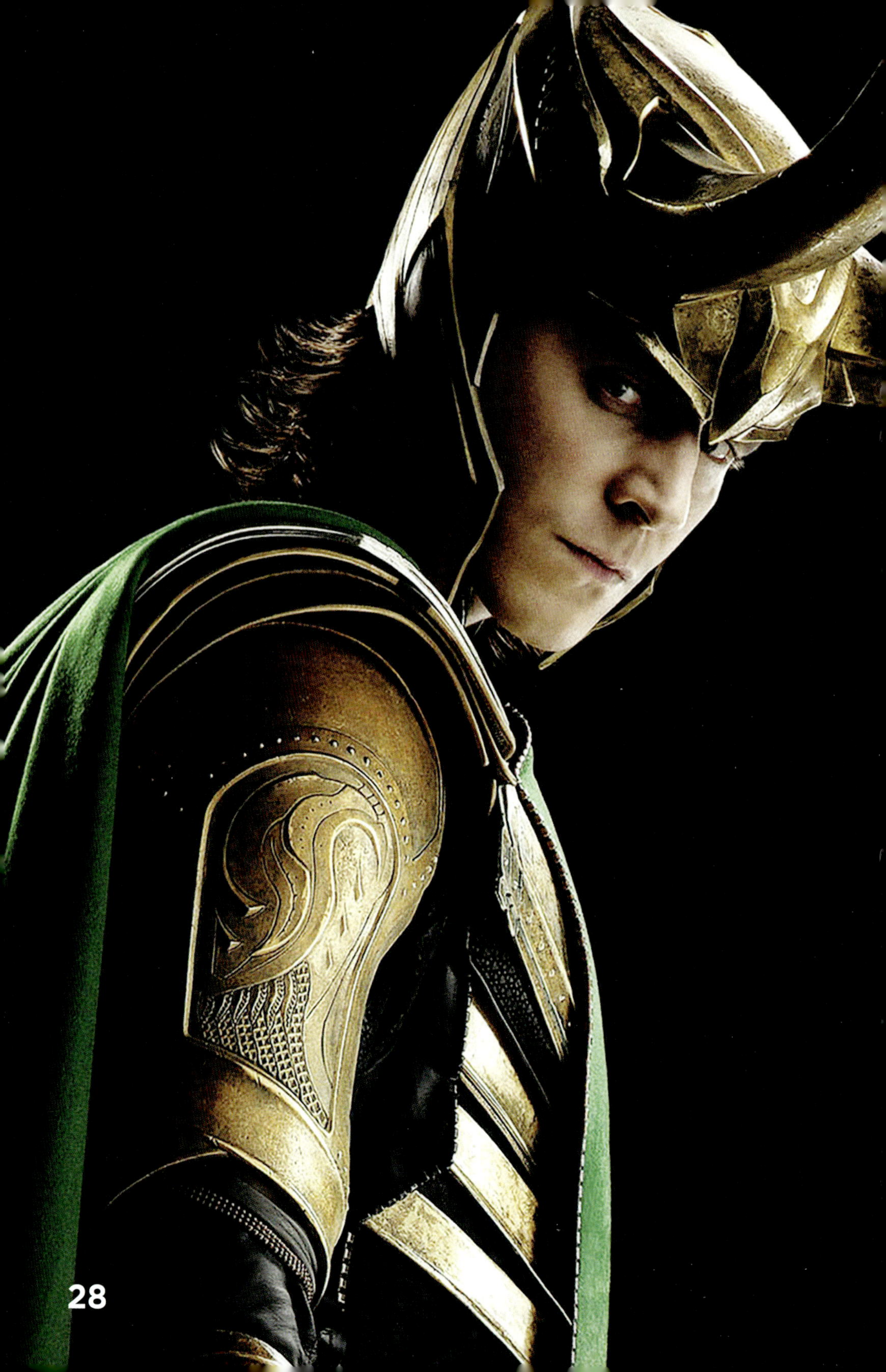

Loki Today

Most Norse stories were spoken. But many years ago, people found ancient poems. They told some Norse myths. That is how people know about Loki today.

Norse myths are still popular. And the characters are still seen today. Loki has been in movies, comic books, and video games. His story lives on.

GLOSSARY

ancient (AYN-shunt)—from a time long ago

appearance (uh-PEER-uhns)—the way someone or something looks

mare (MAIR)—a mature female horse

mistletoe (MIS-uhl-toh)—a plant with yellowish flowers and white berries

myth (MITH)—a story told to explain a practice, belief, or natural occurrence

underworld (UHN-der-wurld)—a place where the souls of the dead go

universe (YOO-nuh-vurs)—all of space and everything in it

venom (VEH-num)—a poison made by animals used to kill or injure

weep (WEEP)—to cry out of sadness

LEARN MORE

BOOKS

Napoli, Donna Jo. *Treasury of Norse Mythology: Stories of Intrigue, Trickery, Love, and Revenge.* Washington, D.C.: National Geographic, 2015.

Shecter, Vicky Alvear. *Thor Speaks!: A Guide to the Viking Realms by the Nordic God of Thunder.* Secrets of the Ancient Gods. Honesdale, PA: Boyds Mills Press, 2015.

Thompson, Ben. *Guts & Glory: The Vikings.* New York: Little, Brown and Company, 2015.

WEBSITES

Middle Ages: Vikings
www.ducksters.com/history/middle_ages_vikings.php

Ten Facts about the Vikings
www.ngkids.co.uk/history/10-facts-about-the-vikings

Vikings: Beliefs and Stories
www.bbc.co.uk/schools/primaryhistory/vikings/beliefs_and_stories/

INDEX

A

ancient Norse, 8, 10–11, 24–25, 29

appearance, 14, 16–17, 18

C

children, 18, 22–23

Fenrir, 22–23

Hel, 22–23

Midgard Serpent, 21, 22–23

P

personality, 4, 7, 13, 26

punishments, 12

T

tricks, 4, 7, 12, 13, 14, 20, 26